DATE DUE

NOV 1 1 1998		
DEC 0 9 1998		

Z8780

BORROWER'S NAME | ROOM NUMBER

BROKEN ARROW BOY

WRITTEN AND ILLUSTRATED BY

ADAM MOORE

and his friends

LANDMARK EDITIONS, INC.

P.O. Box 4469 • 1402 Kansas Avenue • Kansas City, Missouri 64127

Dedicated to:
my mom, Rebecca, my dad, Paul,
and my brothers, Ryan and Tyler;
and to all my wonderful relatives, friends,
teachers, doctors, nurses, therapists,
and everyone else
who helped me along the way.

My deepest thanks to:
Dr. David Fell, Nurse Kellie Cyrus,
Dr. Kathryn Govaerts,
Jeffrey Hammontree "Piginbush",
and my special friend, Bill Murray.

COPYRIGHT © 1990 BY ADAM MOORE

International Standard Book Number: 0-933849-24-9 (LIB.BDG.)

Library of Congress Cataloging-in-Publication Data
Moore, Adam, 1979-
  Broken arrow boy / written and illustrated by Adam Moore.
   p.   cm.
  Summary: Adam Moore describes how he suffered a serious brain injury and
recovered with medical help and family support.
  ISBN 0-933849-24-9 (lib. bdg.)
  1. Moore, Adam, 1979 — Health — Juvenile literature.
  2. Brain — Wounds and injuries — Patients — Oklahoma — Broken
  Arrow — Biography — Juvenile literature.
  [1. Moore, Adam, 1979-
  2. Brain — Wounds and injuries — Patients.
  3. Children's writings.]
  I. Title.
RD594.M66   1990   362.1'97481'0092 — dc20   90-5933
[B]   CIP
[92]   AC

Editorial Coordinator: Nancy R. Thatch
Creative Coordinator: David Melton

Printed in the United States of America

Landmark Editions, Inc.
P.O. Box 4469
1402 Kansas Avenue
Kansas City, Missouri 64127
(816) 241-4919

BROKEN ARROW BOY

When the editors at Landmark and I read the book Adam Moore had entered in the 1989 Contest, all of us were extremely touched by his story. We admired Adam's determination to overcome the handicaps his accident had caused. And we were impressed that he had written his story in such a matter-of-fact way — never asking for sympathy or trying to manipulate the reader's emotions. We felt privileged that he had shared his personal feelings and reactions with us. We also loved his marvelous sense of humor. Landmark Editions is proud to publish BROKEN ARROW BOY in our Gold Award line.

Adam lived and wrote his story, and he created all the pencil illustrations. But because of the unusual nature of the book, we have also included photographs taken by other people and comments made by doctors, nurses, teachers and family members. We feel these add important information and enhance Adam's documentary of remarkable courage.

One of the real pluses in publishing books by children is that our student authors and their families become an extension of our work at Landmark. In turn, our staff becomes an extension of their families. It is certainly a privilege to be included in the Moore Family. And we are pleased to share their extraordinary experiences with those children and adults who have the great fortune to read BROKEN ARROW BOY.

— David Melton
Creative Coordinator
Landmark Editions, Inc.

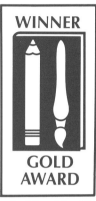

WINNER

GOLD
AWARD

1989

I got a new bicycle for my eighth birthday, April 12, 1987. I planned to ride the wheels off of it during the summer. But I didn't get to do that. You'll see why.

BROKEN ARROW BOY

If you live in Oklahoma, you may have read about me in the newspaper or seen me on television. No, I'm not a movie actor or a television star. I'm just an average, ordinary kid — except some people say I have a weird sense of humor. They're probably right.

My name is Adam Moore. But I'm often called the *Broken Arrow Boy,* and for a couple of good reasons. First of all, I live in Broken Arrow, Oklahoma. And secondly, when I was at Cub Scout Camp one summer, I fell and ran an arrow into my head.

If you're interested in knowing what happened to a kid who had an arrow in his head, you'll probably like this book. But if the thought of a little blood makes you sick at your stomach, perhaps you had better read some other book. My story is definitely not for sissies. You'll soon understand what I mean.

Gray Fox Speaks

Even as a little kid, I wanted to one day become a Boy Scout. When I was a first grader, I was in Indian Guides. The meetings were a lot of fun. We wore feathered headdresses and had Indian names. I was called *Gray Fox*.

At that time my brother, Ryan, who is two years older than I, was a Cub Scout. His Scout shirt was covered with achievement arrows and rank badges. I thought it looked really neat. Sometimes I would sneak into Ryan's closet, put on the shirt, and look at myself in the mirror. The sight made me want to earn even more arrow points when I became a Cub Scout.

Ryan had earned many of his points at Cub Scout Summer Day Camp. And he had a lot of fun there too. So I was eager to attend this camp. When I was eight years old, I enrolled.

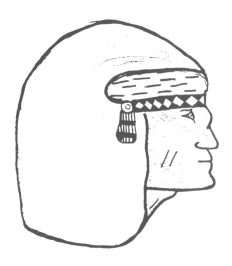

An Indian chieftain is the symbol of Indian Springs Elementary School. Broken Arrow, Oklahoma, is about fifteen miles southeast of Tulsa.

4

Camp started the week after school was out. It was held at the Tulsa Fairgrounds. The first day was sunny and bright, and I couldn't wait to get started. The outdoor games were great fun, especially Red Rover and the relay races.

We also swam at the nearby Big Splash Water Park. I liked that! I did well on my swimming test. I made the top group, so I didn't have to wear a life jacket.

I wanted to earn all of the Cub Scout rank badges.

But the rest of the week wasn't much fun. On the second day, it rained. We had to do all activities inside at the main shelter. Then it rained the next two days. What a bore!

June 12, 1987 — It Happens!

By Friday I didn't want to go to camp at all. But Mom said I should always finish what I start. And I did want to earn those points. So I agreed to go. On the way to camp, the clouds cleared. When I saw the sunshine, things definitely started to look up.

That afternoon the BB gun and archery targets were set up outside. Even though I wasn't a very good marksman, archery was one of my favorite activities. I liked to watch the yellow arrows fly like rockets.

After we had shot our final round, I walked to the target and gathered up my arrows. As I started back to to the firing line, I held the arrows with their points down for safety, just as we had been instructed to do. Then it happened. Suddenly I either slipped or tripped, and I fell forward. When I hit the ground, one of the arrows hit my left eye and went into my head. I remember hearing a soft noise like a — SQUISH!

Then I heard the other boys yelling, "Come quick! Someone's been hurt!"

I started yelling too. I was scared because I knew I was really hurt. I grabbed the arrow and tried to pull it out. After that I don't remember much of what happened. Later I was told that I asked my archery teacher if I had a lot of blood on my shirt. She said I wasn't bleeding very much.

Archery was one of my favorite outdoor activities at camp.

5

When I saw the arrow sticking out of Adam's head, I felt sick. I thought my brother was going to die.

Ryan Moore
Older Brother

When I first saw Adam, he was lying on a stretcher in the Emergency Room. The feathered end of an arrow was projecting from his left upper eyelid. He was very calm and cooperative as I examined him and asked him to perform various things to test his brain function. He seemed to listen carefully when I told him I would have to operate to remove the arrow. Adam was so brave. He would have been an inspiration to all adults.

David A. Fell, M.D., F.A.C.S.
Neurological Surgeon

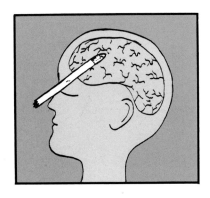

During the surgery a member of the operating team kept Adam's mother and me informed. She phoned and told us when Adam had been given the anesthesia. At one point, she said, "Okay, we've got him opened up now, and we can see the arrow." It was very reassuring for us to know that Adam was still alive.

Paul Moore
Father

The camp director and an off-duty policeman rushed me to a nearby hospital. On the way they kept telling me not to pull at the arrow anymore. To keep me awake, they had me count to five again and again. And they had me say my name over and over.

I was unconscious by the time Mom and Dad arrived at the hospital. Naturally they were shocked by my condition. Since it was so serious, they decided to have me moved to a larger hospital. Unfortunately, the nurses wheeled my cart down the hall where my parents and other relatives were waiting. My brother, Ryan, really freaked out when he saw that yellow arrow sticking out of my head.

I was taken to St. Francis Hospital in a helicopter. The speedy transportation was important. But I think it was unfair that I had my first ride in a helicopter and didn't even know it.

St. Francis Hospital, Tulsa, Oklahoma.

Good News and Bad News

After examining my injury, Dr. Fell told my parents he had to remove the arrow immediately. The operation lasted more than four hours. When it was over, Dr. Fell said that I was a very lucky boy — the arrow had gone through my eyelid, but it had not hit my eyeball. It had also slipped between two big arteries in my brain without cutting into them. If the arrow had nicked either artery, I would have died quickly. Dr. Fell said he had been able to remove all of the arrow. That was certainly good news.

The bad news was — there would probably be a lot of swelling in my brain for several days. And because the arrow was very dirty, I might get a serious infection. Dr. Fell said it would be three days before he would know how badly my brain had been injured. And he didn't know if I would ever be able to see with my left eye.

After surgery I was placed in the Pediatric Intensive Care Unit (PICU for short). I must have been quite a sight! There were IV's

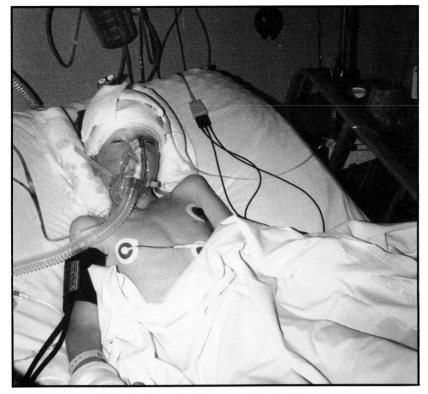

They had me wired for everything but stereo.

I kept thinking, if I hadn't insisted that Adam go to camp that morning, he wouldn't have gotten hurt.

    Rebecca Moore
    Mother

Realizing Adam might not live through the night was very difficult. I felt so helpless. There was nothing I could do to ease Rebecca and Paul's pain. So I prayed to God to please let Adam live.

    Patt Randell
    Maternal Grandmother

(intravenous tubes) stuck in my veins to put nourishment and medicines into my body. And I had wires attached to me so the nurses could monitor my heartbeat and breathing.

While I was in PICU, Mom and Dad stayed with me day and night. But I didn't know it. They held my hand and talked to me, and even sang songs. They hoped I could hear them and know that I wasn't alone.

Code Blue

Two days after the operation, I suddenly stopped breathing. When my nurse called a *Code Blue,* other nurses and doctors came running with special equipment. After they got me to breathe again, Dr. Fell stayed by my side for several hours to make sure I was okay.

But I was not okay. My brain had begun to swell. Dr. Fell told my parents that I would probably die if the swelling didn't stop in the next few minutes. I got lucky again. The swelling stopped.

But in order to keep a constant check on the pressure in my brain, the doctors had to put a bolt into my skull. Now I really looked like Frankenstein's monster. When the pressure went too high, Dr. Fell performed a second operation immediately.

After that operation the pressure in my brain leveled out. But the doctors and nurses were now worried because I didn't wake up. My parents were worried too. They wanted to know if I would ever again be able to see and talk.

After a few days, I finally opened my eyes and looked around for a few minutes. I could see my parents, but they looked blurry. I knew I was in a hospital. And I remembered getting hurt. Then I went right

After the Code Blue, my wife Patt phoned me and said, "I think you had better drive here as soon as possible. And please bring my best dress." That two-hour drive was the longest one I've ever made. I wondered if Adam would still be alive when I got there.

    Hallard Randell
    Maternal Grandfather

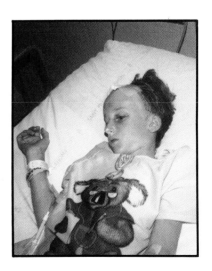

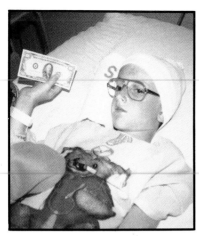

Collecting the big one hundred made my day!

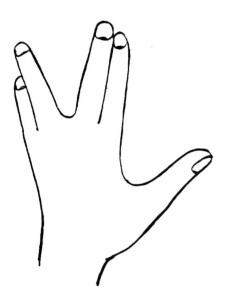

I like taking care of children. They rarely give up. And they seem to be able to ignore pain most of the time. I can't help but get involved with them. I feel joyful when they get better, and I cry when they don't. Then I go home and hug my own kids because I'm thankful they're well.

Kellie Cyrus, R.N.
Pediatric Nurse, PICU

back to sleep. For the next couple of days, I drifted in and out of sleep. Day and night I could hear my parents and the nurses talking to me, telling me I was getting better. I wanted to talk to them too, but I couldn't speak.

Money Talks

Dad decided to make me an offer I couldn't refuse. He knew I liked money. He told me, "Adam, if the first word you say is *Daddy*, I will give you a one-hundred-dollar bill."

When I heard that, I really did want to talk. But I couldn't seem to get my mouth to move right. Then a few days later, I finally made it work. Not being a dumb kid, the first word I whispered was *Daddy*. And I got that hundred-dollar bill. I'd say that's not bad pay for one word. Everyone was thrilled. My being able to speak was an important sign that I was getting better.

Spock Sign

From that point on, I was awake more and more each day. I thought about a lot of things. And it's funny what things you'll think of while lying in a hospital bed. For instance, I remembered watching *Star Trek* with my friends and how annoyed I was when they could make the "Spock sign" better than I could. Now that I had plenty of time, I decided I would practice until I could make the sign perfectly.

After a few days, I could make the best Spock sign in the state of Oklahoma. So I decided it would be a sort of password to my room. Every time a nurse, or anyone else, came in, I raised my hand and made the sign. None of them knew what I was doing. They wondered if something new was wrong with me. But the doctors and nurses were good sports. They started making the sign back at me. That was even funnier because they didn't know what *they* were doing. Some of them were really bad at it, and that tickled me even more. I must admit, I enjoyed having my own little mystery.

But one day a new nurse came in. When I made the sign to her, she said, "You must like *Star Trek* too." My secret was discovered.

The Zombie Kid

Everyone kept telling me how much better I looked and how much I was improving. Although that was a nice thing for them to say, I knew better. I looked like a nightmare on Elm Street. The front half of my head had been shaved for the operation, and I had a long scar from ear to ear. One side of my face was swollen. I still had the bolt in my head. Monitors were stuck on my chest and IV's were inserted in my arms. And the oxygen mask over my nose and mouth made me look like a Top Gun pilot from outer space.

In PICU all the rooms have big glass windows, so the nurses can always see the patients. Only two visitors were allowed in the room at a time. Parents are the only ones who don't need special permission to visit. If the doctor approves, other people can come in. My grandparents, aunts, uncles, and my minister, Walter Buchanon, came to see me often.

Since children were not allowed to visit in PICU, my brothers could not see me. I missed them, and they missed me too. Finally Dr. Fell let them come for a quick visit. When Ryan and Tyler saw me, they tried to act cheerful. But I knew they were surprised by the way I looked.

Let's face it — I wasn't in very good shape. I could breathe and talk a little, but nothing else about me worked very well. I couldn't see with my left eye. I couldn't move my left arm or leg. And when the nurses tickled my left foot or pinched my left hand, I couldn't feel it.

The IV stuck in my arm poured plenty of fluids into my body. But I was still terribly thirsty all the time. Even worse, I didn't have enough energy to ask for a drink of water. So I just lay there like a zombie.

Milk Shake and Whoops!

Finally, one day the nurses let my parents give me a milk shake. That milk shake was better than anything I had ever tasted. And I drank it right down. But as soon as I drank it, I got sick at my stomach and up came the milk shake. Yuck! Okay, I know that's disgusting. But if any kid reading this book has never barfed, then stand on your head and wiggle your ears. Big deal. Here comes more. When I took a sip of water, the same thing happened again.

I had never been a fat kid, but now I was getting skinnier and skinnier by the day. So the doctors decided I should be fed through a tube that was stuck in my nose and run down my throat to my stomach. I found out that wasn't much fun, but I guess it was better than starving.

As I got more nourishment, I started to feel better. A few days later, they took the bolt out of my head. Finally they took the respirator away and I could breathe on my own. But now I had another problem. When I said something, my voice sounded flat like a robot's.

I wasn't able to show emotions either. I didn't laugh. And I didn't cry. When anyone tried to get me to laugh, I would sometimes smile a little. That really worried my parents.

No Chicken Fried Steak!

While I was being fed through a tube, I was still thirsty all the time. And I wanted something to **chew** on, like chicken fried steak — my favorite. But no such luck! The nurses gave my mom some pink star-shaped sponges on the end of sucker sticks. Mom would dip the sponge in water or mouthwash and swish it around in my dry mouth. To me, that sponge tasted great! I thought it looked just like a big, juicy piece of bubble gum. Although Mom told me not to, sometimes I would bite off the sponge part. Then she would have to dig it out of my mouth. I don't think she liked that, but she tried to be really patient with me.

Now, I know what I'm going to say next will sound silly, but I'm going to tell you anyway. One time when I was alone in my room, I

The days and nights at the hospital were exhausting for Paul and me. But it was difficult for us at home too. We would see Adam's friends playing outside, and his brothers were so full of energy. We could hardly stand to go back to the hospital and look at Adam, who was just lying there.

Rebecca Moore
Mother

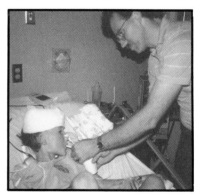

Dad held the milk shake while I gobbled it down.

9

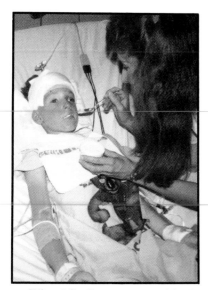

When I finally got to eat real food, I thought it tasted great! (If you look carefully at this picture, you can see the bolt sticking out of the top of my head.)

happened to look over at the brown fuzz-ball nose on my stuffed dog. It looked just like a *Hershey Kiss* to me. And more than anything in the whole world, I wanted to eat it. So I grabbed the dog, and then I bit off its nose and chewed it up. Believe it or not, it didn't taste too bad. I even thought it tasted a little like chocolate.

A couple of days later, Mom noticed the dog and said, "I wonder what happened to that dog's nose?" I acted like I didn't hear her.

As I grew stronger, the doctors decided to let me try to eat again. When the nurse gave me a milk shake and some crackers, I gobbled them down. It was like a gourmet meal! Then everyone waited nervously to see if I would get sick again. I didn't. So after a while I got to try some more food. Dr. Fell said as soon as I could eat full meals, I would be moved to a regular hospital room. I could hardly wait.

Jeff *Piginbush*

One day a physical therapist came to my room. He said he wanted to help me move my left arm and leg. That sounded like a good idea to me. He tried to help me sit up on the side of my bed. But it wasn't easy to do with all the tubes and stuff attached to me. And I was so weak. I had to really concentrate to hold up my head. If the therapist let go, I slumped over, and he would have to catch me. Not being able to sit up by myself worried me. If I couldn't sit up alone, I wondered how I would ever be able to walk again or ride a bicycle.

I work with a lot of kids who have had accidents that could have been avoided. I wish kids would listen when their parents tell them to:

Look both ways before crossing the street!
Don't ride your bikes in traffic!
Buckle your seat belts in the car!
Stay away from storm sewers!
Don't climb on things!
And...STAY AWAY FROM SKATEBOARDS!

I have more patients who are seriously hurt on skateboards than by any other way. Every day I am reminded of how really dangerous the things are. My children will never have skateboards!

Jeffrey Hammontree, R.P.T.
Physical Therapist

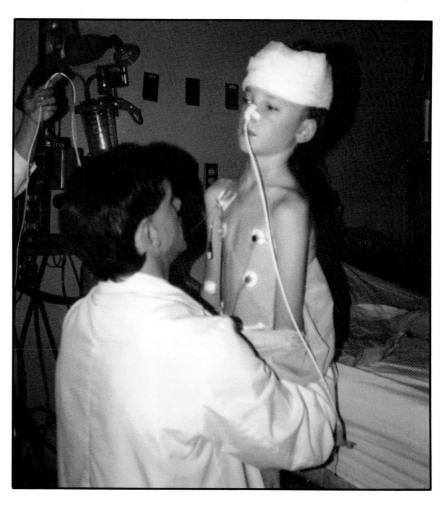

I liked my therapist. His name was Jeffrey Hammontree, and I thought his last name sounded funny. One day my wild sense of humor got charged up, and I teased him.

"You know what, Jeff Hammontree," I said, "I think I'm going to call you Jeff *Piginbush*." And that's what I called him every time I saw him. I still do!

The thing that impressed me most about Adam was his determination to get better. He was willing to do whatever it took to get well.

Jeffrey Hammontree, R.P.T.
Physical Therapist

The Healing Blanket

Oh, I almost forgot to tell about my missing blanket. Now, this may sound like little-kid stuff to you, but it was very important to me. When I was a baby, my grandmother gave a blanket to me. I didn't carry it around with me all the time — the way Linus does in the *Peanuts* comic strip. But my blanket was special to me. For some reason, I believed that blanket had special powers. I called it my "healing blanket."

Whenever I had a wreck on my bicycle, or had a sore muscle, or a bad cut, I would go to bed and wrap my blanket around the hurt place. Soon the pain seemed to go away, and I always felt better the next morning. One day I remembered the blanket. I asked Mom to bring it to the hospital, and she did. I began putting the blanket over my head before I went to sleep. Guess what? I started feeling better.

I don't care what anyone says — I think my healing blanket works!

My blanket happened to be the same shade of green as the hospital sheets. So before the nurses changed my bedding each day, Dad or Mom always removed my blanket. But one time they forgot, and it was carried out with the sheets. When I realized my blanket was gone, I was really upset.

Mom tried to calm me. She promised to find the blanket. She hurried to the big laundry cart, but it was empty. The sheets had already been taken to the laundry room. The laundry staff and the nurses looked for my blanket too. But no one could find it.

Mom gave me a hospital pillowcase to use as a substitute. But it wasn't the same. I was convinced that I would never get well without my blanket.

Finally, Mom went down to the laundry room to look. When she entered the room, she was shocked! Since more than 4,000 pounds of bedding were washed each day, the room was filled! There were folded sheets stacked on the shelves from floor to ceiling.

Knowing how disappointed I would be if she didn't find my blanket, Mom searched for more than an hour. Just as she was about to give up, she happened to notice some stacks of pillowcases. And underneath one of the stacks — there was my blanket! Mom was so excited, she ran all the way back to my room with it. When I put the blanket over my head, I knew I would get better. And I did.

Detective Mom in the hospital laundry room.

Strangers and Other Friends

Now I started looking forward to seeing Jeff "Piginbush" every day. We worked hard at trying to get my left arm and leg to move. I started to eat more too. Soon my brothers were allowed to visit me

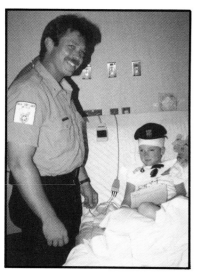

more often. I sure liked that. They drew pictures for me and told me what was going on at home. I told them I planned to get a Nintendo set as soon as I was moved to a regular hospital room. Ryan and Tyler promised to visit often and play games with me.

My other relatives continued to visit, and they often brought presents. And I received more balloons than any other kid in the hospital. My friends and neighbors sent presents and cards, sometimes even money. My bank account grew and grew. But what really surprised me was when I started receiving cards and presents from people who didn't even know me — people who had heard about my accident and wanted to wish me well. I appreciated everyone's kindness.

The Green Beret

One day a man received special permission to see me. His name was Lee Werling. Mr. Werling had been a Green Beret in Vietnam. He told me about being a soldier, and his jokes made me feel good. Before he left he did one of the nicest things. He gave me the green beret he had worn in the war. Then he laid some pins and uniform patches on my chest and saluted me. He said I was very brave — just like a good soldier.

"Adam," he said, "there are three important things I learned while I was a Green Beret: Never say die; never give up; and always finish what you start."

I promised him I would try to do all these things.

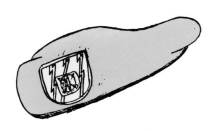

I'm proud of the green beret that Mr. Werling gave to me. And I felt honored to return his salute.

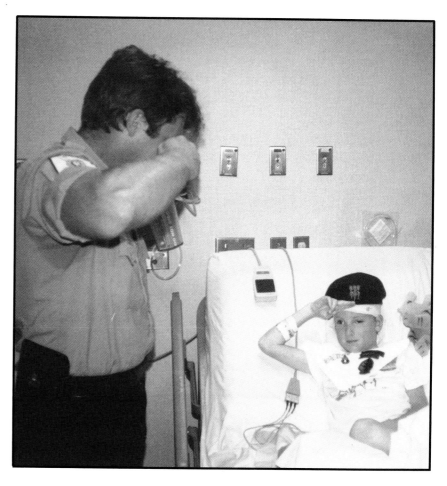

An Awesome Room!

When the day finally arrived for me to leave PICU, I was really excited. I can still remember how wonderful it felt to ride down the hall in my hospital bed to my new room. Now I was in the children's regular wing! Now I had a room of my own!

And, boy, was my room awesome! It had a Snoopy telephone, so I could call my family and friends. There was a television set, and Dad had bought the Nintendo and hooked it up. Special privileges also came with this regular room. Instead of having to wear hospital gowns, I got to wear my own T-shirts. And I could now have visitors other than family members.

I even got to choose my own foods each day! At first I was so hungry, I loved all the hospital food. But I soon tired of it. Sometimes Mom or my aunts would bring in my favorite foods — slushies, donuts, and best of all, *Kraft* macaroni and cheese. I loved that! My hands still didn't work very well so people had to feed me. But as my condition improved, I kept trying to feed myself. After a while I could use a spoon and a fork fairly well.

Next Time, He'll Believe Me

One morning Jeff "Piginbush" came in with a wheelchair and said he was going to take me to the therapy room. What a treat! He helped me get out of bed and took me for my first wheelchair ride.

Jeff said I needed to work hard to teach my muscles to function again. The exercises were tough to do. Because of the injury to my brain, I had not used my arms and legs for a long time. My muscles had tightened — especially those in my legs. When Jeff stretched my legs, they hurt.

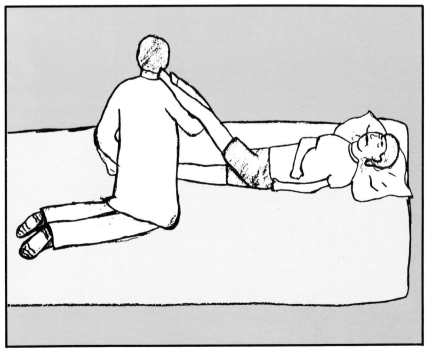

"Come on, Adam, relax your leg," Jeff would say. "Just a little bit more. You can do it."

When Adam came out of intensive care, he still spoke in a flat, robotlike voice. And he didn't laugh. He didn't cry. He didn't show any emotions. We knew he recognized his father, his brothers, and me, but he showed no indication that he loved us. That scared me more than anything. I was afraid we had really lost him.

Rebecca Moore
Mother

My first ride in a wheelchair.

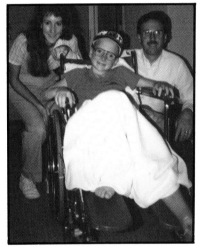

Hospital food got to be a bore.

Adam once said that I was his "worst nightmare." I have no doubt he tried to catch me off guard with that statement. Well, he did — he definitely hit the mark he wanted to hit. I had to consider if I was pushing him too hard or causing him too much pain. Perhaps I needed to back off a little and let him improve more gradually. I think Adam knew that I was sensitive enough to consider these things. But at the same time, I had to keep in mind how important it was to maintain the intensity of Adam's therapy, in order for him to return to a normal life as soon as possible.

Jeffrey Hammontree, R.P.T.
Physical Therapist

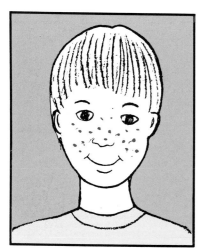

Where did all the freckles go?

When the pain was really bad, I would talk to Jeff to try to distract him. Sometimes I told him jokes, hoping he would forget to stretch my legs as many times. I was willing to try anything to get him to stop! One day I told him if he pulled my legs again, I would get sick at my stomach. But I didn't. And he knew I was only teasing.

Several days later when I told him I was sick, he said, "Oh, Adam, you're just trying to trick me again!" But he soon found out I wasn't fooling — I threw up all over him. I thought he would be angry, but he wasn't. He just changed into clean clothes. Jeff and I laugh about it now, but I don't think he thought it was so funny then.

Everyone Has Accidents

One night I told Mom that I was mad at myself for having fallen on that arrow. I knew I had caused a lot of trouble for everyone.

"You shouldn't be mad at yourself," she said. "It was an accident. Everyone has accidents. Some accidents are small ones and some are big ones. You just happened to have a big one. We can't change things that have already happened."

The Vampire Squad

Although I was now in a regular room, I still had to have IV's to take lots of special medicines through my veins. That meant needles! And I hated needles more than anything because they hurt me.

The nurses had to put the needles into a vein in my wrist. And since I have tiny veins, it was difficult for them to find one that was big enough. They usually had to poke several times to find the right place. Worse still, an IV needle could be left in one spot for only a few days because that area would start getting red and tender. Then the nurses would have to remove the old needle and put another one in another vein. I often screamed and yelled because it hurt so much. Most of the nurses were nice to me, but I always hated to see them come in to check my IV's. I called them the *Vampire Squad*.

The Disappearing Freckles

The needles weren't my only problem. Some of the medicines that came through the IV's were really strong, and they stung my arms like fury. Others made me sick. One medicine caused a bright red, itchy rash that lasted for days. Then there was another medicine that caused something funny to happen to my freckles. I have a lot of them and I always wondered what I would look like without them. Well, I got the chance to find out. The medicine made all my freckles disappear! That was fun — for a while. After a few months, they all came back and I was as speckled as ever.

IV's and Wheelchairs

Most of the other kids on the children's floor had IV's attached to their arms too. When they got up to walk or ride in wheelchairs, their IV bags were hung on a machine that rolled along beside them.

There was a special game room on the children's floor. As I got better, I was allowed to go there in my wheelchair. I liked the pool

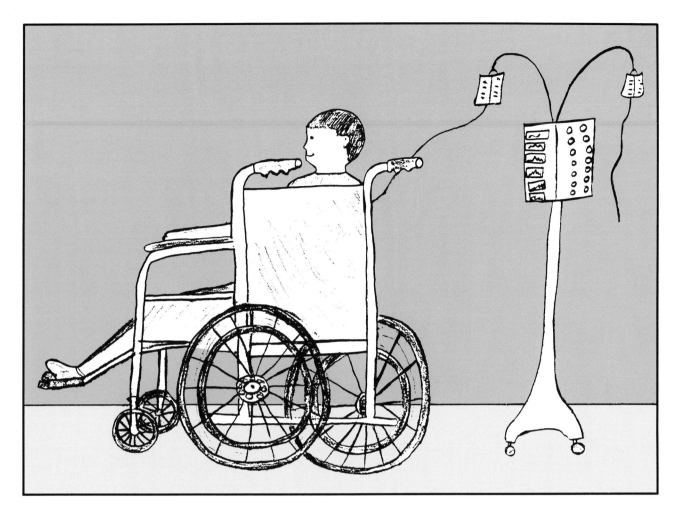

table best of all. Since my left hand wasn't working yet, I couldn't use a cue stick. So I had to roll the balls with my good hand. I could always find another kid who wanted to play the game with me.

"When Can I Go Home?"

As the days wore on, I really got tired of being in the hospital. Every time Dr. Fell came in, I asked him, "When can I go home?"

"You may go as soon as you're able to take your medicine in pills and no longer need an IV machine," he would reply.

Dr. Fell kept his promise. After I started taking pills, he came into my room one day and said, "Adam, how would you like to go home tomorrow?"

I was so excited, I couldn't sleep that night. It was hard for me to believe that I would soon be back at my own house, in my own room, with my own toys, and with my own family and friends. I knew my dog Misty and my parakeets would be glad to see me.

Morning finally came. I was so happy when I climbed into the wheelchair. As I said good-bye to my nurses, I promised that one day I would give them a real surprise. I would **walk** up to visit them!

It was a hot, bright summer day. I had not been outside for a long time and the sunshine felt friendly on my face. Besides, it was July 18 — my younger brother Tyler's fifth birthday. I was looking forward to helping him celebrate.

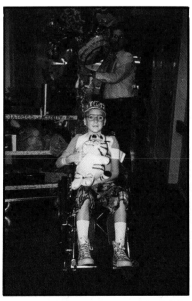

I still couldn't express myself very well, but underneath my very straight face was a great big smile. Dad got to carry the balloons. He had a wild time trying to get them all into the car.

15

But I was worried too. I wondered how my friends would react when they saw me. I wore a hat so they couldn't see the scar across my head or tell that I had the weirdest looking haircut in the world. Let's just say, I looked stranger than a punk rocker.

Surprise!

As the car turned onto my street, I saw lots of kids and grownups in my front yard. What a great surprise! Our neighbors had come to welcome me home. They had painted signs and hung them on our house. They also brought presents for me. And there were balloons everywhere I looked.

As my parents helped me into the wheelchair, everyone crowded around and told me I looked really great. I guess I did, considering everything that had happened to me. It made me feel good that everyone was so happy to see me again. Without a doubt, it was the best day of the summer!

All the excitement soon made me tired. When I lay down to take a nap, my own bed felt wonderful. I woke up just in time to go to Tyler's birthday party at *McDonald's*. Since I hadn't been anywhere in such a long time, I could hardly wait to get there. Seeing Tyler's friends made it seem like old times. But I didn't stay very long. After a few minutes, I got tired and had to go home.

Thermo Man

It was a lot of work for my parents to take care of me at home. Besides renting a wheelchair, they rented a hospital bed and set it downstairs in their bedroom. It was necessary for me to be near them. They had to give me medicines, day and night, and check my temperature every hour. My temperature went up and down frequently. Every day it varied between 97 degrees and 104 degrees. I had to take an aspirin every four hours. Dad took my temperature so many times, I nicknamed him *Thermo Man*.

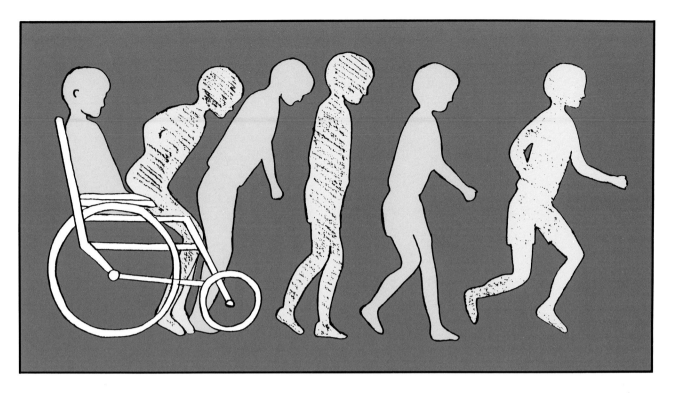

"Move, Leg!"

After I had been home a few days, I wanted to try to walk. Dad helped me stand up in the living room. He stayed right behind me so I wouldn't fall.

"Come on, leg — do your stuff!" I said. Then I tried to make my left leg move, but it wouldn't. It just stayed still. I was desperate.

"Move!" I commanded.

And do you know what? For the first time since the accident, my left leg moved forward and I took a few steps. But I was so wobbly I started to fall. Then somehow my brain and my body knew what to do next. I began to run. It worked! When I ran I could keep my balance. My parents and brothers couldn't believe their eyes as they watched me run around and around the couch. They were so happy, they jumped up and down, clapped their hands, and laughed and cheered.

I worked hard every day to improve my walking. But I could walk for only short periods of time. I still had to use my wheelchair to get around in the house. I certainly needed it when I went outside.

"Faster! Faster!"

My brothers thought my wheelchair was neat. They argued over who would get to ride in it when I wasn't using it. They could make it go really fast and turn it quickly. But Mom didn't like all the racket, so after a few days, the wheelchair was made off limits to anyone but me.

Learning to maneuver a wheelchair takes some time. At first I had to be pushed because my left arm was in a sling due to my weak shoulder. Even learning to push someone in a wheelchair isn't easy. It took Mom a while to get the hang of it. Until she did, I got banged

Before the accident Adam and I were pretty good friends. Of course, we fought like brothers do, but we liked each other. Adam was smart and fun to be around. But when he came home, he wasn't the same. He couldn't walk. And he didn't have much concentration. He got tired quickly. If we played a game, he wouldn't play for very long. I didn't think Adam would ever be like he was before the accident.

Ryan Moore
Older Brother

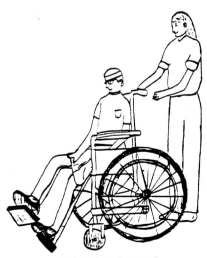

Pedestrians Beware!

17

into a lot of curbs and stuck in several doorways. And sometimes I had to remind her to put on the brake. I teased her about being a reckless driver.

I must say, I admire my mom! The wheelchair was heavy for her to load in and out of the car, but she never complained once. I had many doctor appointments. And three times a week, Mom drove me to Tulsa for my physical therapy at the Children's Medical Center. She tried to make these outings enjoyable for me too. On the way home, we would sometimes stop for pizza or go to a nice restaurant. When we went to a movie, I got to sit in the aisle in my wheelchair. That was neat.

A Time To Remember

The first Sunday I was able to go back to church was a time I will never forget. When my family entered the church door, the minister came straight to me and helped me walk to the front of the congregation. He told everyone how pleased he was that I was able to return to church.

About 900 people were there that day. I had never before been in front of that many people. Everyone clapped for me! And no one had ever clapped in church before. That made me feel very special. I felt grateful too. I knew the members had said many prayers for me. I believe those prayers helped me to survive.

A Lot of Hard Work

At the Children's Medical Center, the therapists showed me how to do exercises to strengthen my weak left side. I worked hard to improve my balance, and I began to walk longer distances. Although my legs hurt when I exercised them, I could tell I was getting stronger and walking better. When I tried my best, my therapists let me do something I liked — such as jumping on the trampoline or playing games with them.

Thirty minutes before the neighborhood pool opened each day, Mom or Dad could take me swimming. I loved to swim because I could move easily in the water and my body felt normal.

On one of my visits to the Children's Medical Center, I met Dr. Govaerts, a child psychologist. She talked to me about my accident, then tested me to find out how much school work I remembered. Except for math, the tests weren't too difficult. Dr. Govaerts and my parents were pleased with my scores.

My Room At Last!

Finally, I got to move upstairs and into my own room. I was happy to find all my stuff was just the way I had left it. I was afraid Tyler might have messed it up. But he had been a good kid.

Before my accident Tyler and I had been busy with our own friends. But now that I had to stay inside the house so much, we started spending a lot of time together. And we became real pals.

I saved all the metallic balloons I had received. Mom pinned the balloons on my ceiling so I could look at them when I went to bed.

Dad and I felt like we had our own private swimming pool.

The results of the tests Adam took showed he remembered a lot of information he had known before the accident. That meant we had a good foundation to build upon. That was a real plus.

Kathryn Govaerts, Ph.D.
Pediatric Psychologist

Although I enjoyed my room, I had trouble sleeping up there alone. I would wake up during the night and be frightened. Mom or Dad would have to come up and carry me downstairs to their room.

Back to the Hospital

On Dad's birthday in August, I had to go back to the hospital. Of course, the "Vampire Squad" and their needles were waiting for me. My blood tests showed that the medicine I was taking to protect me from having seizures was beginning to damage my liver. I was given a different medicine. I stayed in the hospital for a week to see how I reacted to it. I did okay.

Blast Off!

While I was there, other tests were made too. I didn't mind most of them. In fact, I liked some of them, especially the x-rays. And I liked the CT (Computer Thermography) scan too, where a huge x-ray machine took a picture of my brain.

St. Francis Hospital also had a Magnetic Resonance Imaging (MRI) machine. The MRI used magnets to take x-rays of my brain. Mom could go into the room with me. But she had to take off all her jewelry because the machine's magnets pulled any metallic objects toward it.

The first time I saw the MRI, I was amazed. It was in a big room that looked like a Star Wars chamber. When I was placed on the MRI table and strapped in, the table slid into the machine automatically. There was a mirror inside, so I could see myself. I couldn't move at all. But I could talk by way of a special speaker to the person who was doing the test. I liked to pretend that I was in a spaceship getting ready to blast off into outer space.

I liked having Adam home. He played games with me, instead of going out with his friends. We had a lot of fun. I liked helping him and getting things for him.

Tyler Moore
Younger Brother

When Adam came home, I didn't think he would ever have to go back to the hospital. I thought he would stay home and our family would get back to normal. But it didn't work out that way.

Ryan Moore
Older Brother

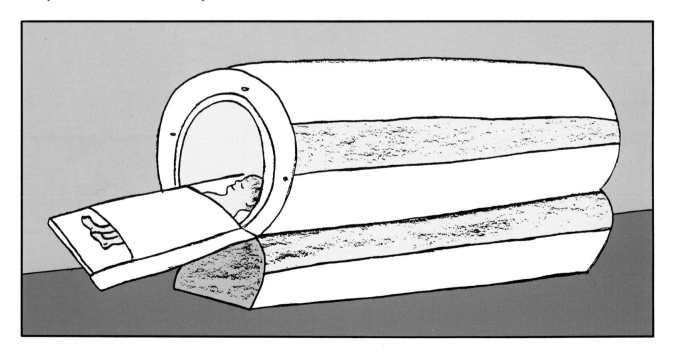

The machine made a lot of noise. It sounded like a jackhammer. Strange as it may seem, the noise always put me to sleep. The whole test took about an hour, but it was fun and didn't hurt at all.

My "ticker" looked great on the screen.

When I started teaching Adam, not all of his hair had grown back. But the scars didn't look too bad. Even so, Adam was embarrassed and preferred to wear a hat so no one could see the top of his head. He was eager to start on his lessons. He was worried that he would never catch up with his classmates.

Mary Emerson
Homebound Teacher

It was good to know that I could still do something right.

I also had an interesting test done on my heart. It was called a Sonogram. I could see my insides on a color screen and watch my heart as it beat. That was really neat!

But there were other tests I didn't like. I particularly hated the blood tests because I didn't like having my fingers stuck with the you-know-what's. And I didn't like the Electroencephalogram (EEG) either. This test recorded my brain wave patterns on graph paper. The main problem with the EEG was that it was messy. A bunch of little wires were attached to my head. Each wire had a plastic piece on the end, with gooey stuff on it so it would stick to my head. The goo, of course, got in my hair, and it smelled awful. And removing the wires pulled my hair, and that hurt. Ouch!

Mom and Dad weren't allowed to stay with me while I took an EEG. That made me dislike the test even more. But after I got really upset about it one day, the nurse told my parents they could stay with me the next time. That taught me an important thing — if you tell your doctors and nurses that something really bothers you, they'll try to bend the rules whenever they can.

Everyone Else Goes Back to School

In the fall I wasn't strong enough to go to school. But my teacher saved a desk for me. And my classmates sent lots of cards to me and wrote letters about what was happening at school.

On October 14 I was finally allowed to return to school. I was so happy to see everyone, and I looked forward to a whole day in school. But I grew very tired and didn't feel well. I also had trouble understanding some things. That made me even more nervous. To make things worse, my eyes were sensitive to light and any kind of noise bothered me. I had to go home after lunch.

As time went on, the situation didn't get any better. I ended up attending class for only a part of each day. Finally I had to stay home. But on the bright side, the school arranged to have a teacher come to our house several times a week. Her name was Mary Emerson, and I liked her immediately. With her help, I kept up with my studies. And she told wonderful stories about other homebound students and joked with me a lot. If I was having a bad day, she was very understanding and would come back at another time.

A Winner!

I also started going back to Cub Scout meetings. But I had to miss a lot of fun activities, such as field trips. My den mother sent crafts home for me to work on. Making a pinewood derby car was my most exciting project. I was really proud of that car. It won a third place trophy at the Pack Meeting Race.

Trick or Treat

Halloween is the time for spooks and goblins, and trick or treat. All the kids in the neighborhood were buying costumes. But I didn't want a store-bought outfit. I wanted a costume that was completely different. And I had a great idea for one.

My dad laughed when I told him what I wanted to wear. (He's got a weird sense of humor too.) But Mom didn't think it was funny at all. It took a lot of talking before she agreed to let me do it. All of us promised to keep my costume a secret.

The day before Halloween, Mom took me to a party supply store. We bought the very thing I needed to make my costume complete. I could hardly wait to see the neighbors' reactions to it.

On the big night, I dressed in my Cub Scout uniform. Then I opened the box and took out the special thing I had bought. I couldn't help but giggle when I placed the thing on my head. I was wearing one of those fake arrows. And it looked like I had an arrow **sticking through my head!**

I admired Adam in so many ways. But I think I was most impressed by his sense of humor. His Halloween costume bowled me over. What a kid!

Carlotta Rose, R.N.
Clinical Nurse II, Pediatrics

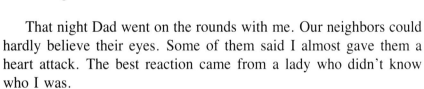

Ryan is in the dog costume. Tyler is the pirate. I bet you can guess who has the arrow through his head.

That night Dad went on the rounds with me. Our neighbors could hardly believe their eyes. Some of them said I almost gave them a heart attack. The best reaction came from a lady who didn't know who I was.

"It looks like you had better go to the hospital and get that arrow taken out!" she said.

"I already have!" I replied.

Dad and I had a big laugh about that. I wanted to trick-or-treat all night, but soon I got tired and had to return home. It was still the best Halloween I have ever had.

Something's Wrong!

I hoped the worst of my illness was behind me. I had suffered a bad accident, but I had survived it. I thought I would continue to get better from now on. I was wrong. In November I started getting sick again. I had terrible headaches. They were so bad they made me sick at my stomach. At night I would wake up with a headache, then run to the bathroom and throw up. I felt even worse during the daytime.

Adam was always a giggler. And he had one of the most contagious laughs. When he laughed, everyone who heard him couldn't help but laugh too. Halloween was wonderful. As I listened to Adam giggle and laugh that night, it was like having the old Adam back.

Paul Moore
Father

It is devastating to have something like this happen to a grandchild. We not only hurt for Adam, but for Paul and Rebecca too. We wanted to protect them from the pain and worry, but we couldn't. So we did what we could to help. We took care of Ryan and Tyler and tried to make everyday life run as smoothly as possible. We will always be proud of Paul and Rebecca for the strength and courage they maintained throughout such a difficult time.

Tom and Sue Moore
Paternal Grandparents

My headaches were terribly painful. My head felt like it was splitting apart!

Cerebrospinal fluid is a clear liquid that surrounds the brain and spinal cord and cushions them from damage. If too much of the fluid builds up in the skull, it can cause extreme pressure.

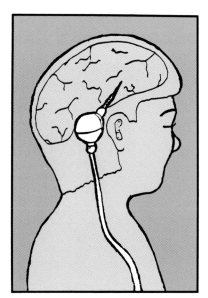

The shunt.

At first Dr. Fell thought I might have a flu, but I didn't. He sent me to Dr. Steve Miller, a neurologist who specializes in treating children with brain problems. Dr. Miller thought I might have too much pressure pushing against my brain. He gave me some medicine, but it didn't help. And since I couldn't eat very much, I started losing weight again.

More doctor visits! More tests! More needles! More troubles! The tests showed that a cerebrospinal fluid build-up in my skull was causing the pressure. Dr. Fell said he would have to put a shunt in the side of my head to drain off the fluid.

A *shunt* in my head? That didn't sound too swift to me.

"Will people be able to see it?" I asked him.

"No, Adam, the shunt will be placed behind your ear," he explained as he handed me one to look at. "As you can see, the shunt is a little round valve with a tiny rubber tube attached to it. The tube will be run down your neck and chest, just under the skin, and into your stomach. This way, the extra fluid can flow through the tube and drain into your stomach."

I sure didn't want to go back to the hospital, but I hated being sick at my stomach even worse. One day I threw up twenty times.

The Surprise Telephone Call

On February 7, the day before I returned to the hospital, I was really feeling low. About noon the telephone rang. The call was for me. It was Bill Murray — one of the stars of *Ghostbusters*. Boy, was I surprised!

He called me from Hollywood where he was making the movie, *Scrooged*. We talked for a long time. He was funny and made me laugh a lot. Mr. Murray liked to play Nintendo games too. But he had been too busy to try out his newest ones. He promised to send them to me. I was so excited by his call that I almost forgot I had to go back to the hospital.

Bill Murray proved he was a man of his word. Just before we left for the hospital the next morning, a package arrived with two Nintendo games inside. I took them with me. I wanted to play them as soon as I got out of surgery.

The operation wasn't too bad. When I woke up in the recovery room, Mom and Dad were there. I felt pretty good — just a little sore and uncomfortable. But pain medicine and *7UP* took care of that.

Back and Forth

I stayed in the hospital for five days. But as soon as I got home, I started feeling sick again. I had another terrible headache and a sick stomach. This really upset me. I wondered why the operation hadn't worked. The doctors had said it would.

For the next few months, it was back and forth to the hospital. On March 9 the doctors installed a new shunt with a different pressure valve. But after I went home, I still felt bad.

Now I was really scared because I knew I wasn't getting well. And I dreaded the idea of going back to the hospital. For a while I tried to act like I felt better than I really did. Then I got the worst stomach ache ever, and I couldn't pretend any longer. On March 22 Mom and Dad rushed me to the Emergency Room. So there I was again — IV's stuck in my arm and eating hospital food!

Something was wrong with me all right. The area where the shunt drained into my stomach had become infected. Dr. Fell operated and removed that part of the shunt. Then a small hole was cut in my head, just behind my ear, so the fluid could drain out through a tube and into a small plastic bag.

After my stomach had healed, he operated on March 30 and put a new shunt inside. After each operation my stomach was really sore, but at least the sharp pain was gone.

During these stays at the hospital, I had even more visitors. But there were days when I was too tired to talk to them. Sometimes I would want visitors, and no one would show up. Other days I didn't want to see people, and in they would come. Sometimes I was embarrassed because I was so pale and thin. And if I didn't know the visitor very well, I worried that my covers might slip off or that I would have to go to the bathroom.

One thing for sure — I wanted Mom or Dad with me every minute. But they couldn't stay all the time. Dad had to work and Mom had to take care of my brothers. So some of our friends and people from church began taking turns staying with me. They read to me, showed me how to draw, and played games with me. My grandparents were wonderful too. They often came to see me. They were the next best thing to having Mom and Dad there.

My friend Bill Murray. He still phones to ask how I am.

I've never seen a more stable family in my life. Whenever Adam's parents brought him back to the hospital, his mother would smile and say, "Well, we're here again. The shunt's not working." And Adam would start playing Nintendo, as if to say, "Oh, well, another surgery."

Suzi Siegler, R.N.
Magnetic Resonance Imaging Department

Paul and I felt we were living in a twilight zone. We had trouble functioning outside the hospital. At one point, Paul felt he wasn't doing more than fifteen minutes of productive work a day at his office. He offered to let his partner take over the company. But his partner wouldn't even consider it. He said, "You take care of Adam and I'll take care of the business." Paul's partner is a wonderful man.

Rebecca Moore
Mother

23

There were two months of total frustration because the shunts kept failing. The doctors would put in a new one, and everyone would feel hopeful. Then something would go wrong with that one too. As each shunt failed, the glimmer of hope grew dimmer and dimmer. When I went to the hospital to teach Adam, I would notice how frightened he was. Not only was he shrinking physically — he was shrinking emotionally as well.

Mary Emerson
Homebound Teacher

It was a very difficult time for Adam. He had believed the doctors and the other adults when they told him the next operation would take care of his problems. But after he'd had so many operations and didn't get better, Adam stopped trusting anyone.

Kathryn Govaerts, Ph.D.
Pediatric Psychologist

Adam's second stay in the hospital was much worse for him psychologically. He was very weak and thin. And he felt so bad, he often became depressed. One day he said, "It might be easier to lie down in a coffin and get some rest." I knew then that he couldn't take much more.

Rebecca Moore
Mother

Working with sick children isn't easy. But there were only two times I ever considered quitting. One time was with Adam. When his second shunt failed, I entered the hospital room just as the nurses started to take him to the x-ray room. They were going to inject dye into his head to find where the shunt was failing. Adam was so frail and in so much pain that when they picked him up, he began yelling the most blood-curdling screams. It was agonizing for me to witness such severe pain and not be able to relieve it in any way. I could see by the expression on his mother's face that she would gladly have taken all his pain upon herself. At that point I wanted to walk out of the hospital and quit. But I knew Adam wasn't a quitter. And his mother wasn't going to quit either. As long as they kept going, I knew I couldn't walk away.

Mary Emerson
Homebound Teacher

Worrywart

When I finally got home on April 2, I worried even more about getting sick again. I worried about school too. I knew I was getting farther behind in my studies. And I was afraid I might never be able to catch up. My homebound teacher told me the school work could wait. She said I must not worry. The most important thing for me was to get well.

Here We Go Again!

I was home less than one week. Then I got another shunt infection. Mom cried when the doctor said I had to go back to the hospital.

On April 8 the infected shunt was removed. On April 18 a new shunt was put in on the other side of my head, but it didn't work right. The doctor had to add a new part to the shunt, so I had to have another operation on April 27.

More sickness! More needles! More days at the hospital! I was so tired of it all that I became very angry! I was mad at the hospital, mad at the nurses, and mad at the doctors. When Dr. Fell came to my room one day, I reached up, grabbed his tie, and pulled him down! He tried to act like it was a joke, but I think he knew I was running out of patience. **Seven** operations in **seventy-nine** days was enough!

Deep down I realized that the doctors and nurses cared about me and were trying to help me. But I felt like I had no control over my own life. From day to day, I didn't know what anyone was going to do to me. I felt so helpless when the nurses came into my room that I would start to cry. I dreaded the ''Vampire Squad'' most of all.

One day a special nurse came in to talk with me. She brought a puppet and let me stick an IV into its arm. That was fun. You can bet, I poked it real hard. Then, for a change, my nurse let me take her blood pressure. And she gave me some shot needles of my very own to play with. I gave shots to some balloons. POP! POP! POP! Now that was more like it! I began to feel in charge.

But then a terrible loneliness set in. Even when Mom or Dad was with me, I felt lonely. If they telephoned me, I would start crying because I wanted to be at home in my own room.

My Hospital Birthday

I spent my ninth birthday in the hospital. I woke up that morning feeling really sorry for myself. I was sure I wouldn't get any presents, or even a cake. So I cried for a while. Then I watched TV. Then I cried some more.

But in the middle of the morning, a friend from church surprised me. She brought a cake and a real neat T-shirt to me. When the mail arrived, I received lots of cards and three cookie bouquets. Then friends started coming by with presents and lots of balloons. After school was out, my brothers and parents had a party for me. All in all, it was the best birthday I had ever had!

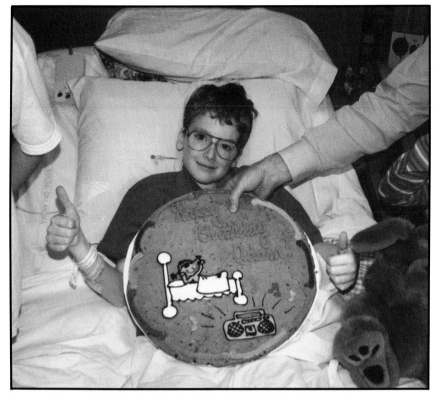

Thumbs up for birthdays, even when they're celebrated in hospitals!

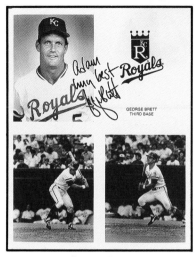

George Brett

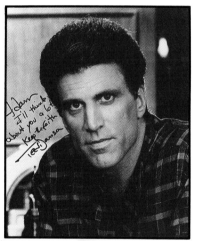

Ted Danson

Mail Call

My favorite time of the day was when the mail arrived. I always got a lot. My hospital room was plastered with cards and letters. When I looked at them, I was reminded that people from all over the country wanted me to get better.

A woman in my church wrote the Kansas City Royals baseball team and told them I was a big fan. The Royals sent a large envelope of stuff to me and an autographed picture of George Brett. Ted Danson, the actor who plays Sam on television's *Cheers,* also sent his autographed picture. And one day I got a big box of seashells from some Cub Scouts in Ocean Grove, New Jersey. The boys of Den 1, Pack 41, had gone to a beach and picked up the shells just for me. I still have all of these things, and I will keep them forever.

When I wasn't too sick, I loved to pass the time making things. Volunteers at the hospital would come into my room and show me how to do crafts. I painted ceramics and made a sun-catcher to hang in my window. I even potted plants.

Craft projects helped pass the time.

Home Again

When I finally got out of the hospital on April 30, I felt I was really getting better. And I was better. A few weeks went by without a single headache. I wanted to go back to school, so Mom arranged it. But I only went a few times. I had missed so much school work, I felt out of place. Instead, I continued to have my lessons at home with Ms. Emerson. I somehow managed to keep up with my class. In May I passed to the Fourth Grade.

It's not easy for a homebound student to stay on grade level, especially one who was as sick as Adam. But he kept up. He must have worked very hard to do it.

Linda Lofton
Third Grade Teacher

The Helmet

I was looking forward to a summer of fun. "Any kind had to be better than the last one!" I told myself. I planned to spend a lot of time outdoors. My bike was waiting for me in the garage. At first I couldn't ride it very well because of my poor balance. And my parents insisted that I wear a helmet. What a bummer! None of the other kids wore a helmet — except my friend Michael Vogt. Sometimes he wore one just to make me feel better. He's a great kid!

Mom was worried that I would get hurt, so she insisted I ride my bike only in front of our house. At first I didn't mind staying close by. But that soon became a drag. I wanted to ride around the corner to our neighborhood playground.

Finally, one fine day Mom gave in and said I could ride to the park. I felt like I had been set free! But as soon as I turned the corner, three boys began to make fun of me.

"Hey, look," one of them said. "He thinks he's really cool wearing that biker's helmet."

I got so upset. I cried all the way home. When Mom saw how upset I was, she went to talk to the boys.

When I rode my bike to the playground a few days later, one of the boys came over, and we played together for awhile. He never mentioned the helmet. That was nice.

Trouble with Tears

Speaking of crying — during this time I had a lot of trouble controlling my tears. I cried several times a day. Usually I didn't know why. I just couldn't help it. It was embarrassing and it worried me. I knew it would be hard to return to school in the fall if I couldn't control my tears. Mom and Dad thought I should discuss the problem with Dr. Govaerts.

I liked talking with Dr. Govaerts. She always made me feel good about myself. She explained that I cried because the arrow had gone into a place in my brain where my emotions are controlled. My brain didn't know when it was all right to cry and when it wasn't. I had retrained my left leg and arm to move properly. Now I needed to retrain my brain about crying. Dr. Govaerts gave me ideas that helped me remember when to cry and when not to. As the summer went by, I didn't cry as often or worry as much.

The Ceremony of the Arrow

For the one-year anniversary of my accident, I wanted to do something special to celebrate getting better. Dad and I came up with a great idea. On June 12 I would take an arrow, break it, and throw it into Grand Lake.

At a sporting goods store we bought an arrow exactly like the one I had used at camp. Some of our friends invited us to spend the weekend at the lake with them. That fit perfectly into our plan. On Sunday we enjoyed riding across the lake in their new boat. If I got hot or tired, I went below and rested. When I had the energy, I sat

When Adam got upset about things other children said to him, he often cried. I had to make him aware that there were other ways he could react. So Adam and I made a list of choices. When a kid said something that upset him, he could:

1. Hit the kid;
2. Run and hide;
3. Tell his mother or his teacher;
4. Tell the kid's mother or father; or
5. Give the kid an *I-can't-believe-you-said-that* look.

Adam practiced that look until he had it down pat. Many times the look saved him from running away or crying.

Kathryn Govaerts, Ph.D.
Pediatric Psychologist

Ryan, Tyler, and I got ready for the Ceremony of the Arrow.

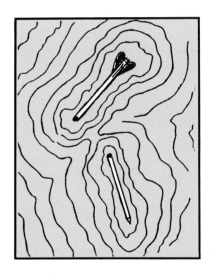

on top, let the wind blow against my face, and waved to people on passing boats. I waited patiently for the afternoon to come. I wanted my arrow ceremony to take place at the same time my accident had occurred.

In the afternoon we pulled into a cove and dropped anchor. At exactly 3:45, I walked to the front of the boat. When my dad handed the arrow to me, I held it in both hands. Then I broke it across my knee and threw the pieces into the lake. We watched as they drifted across the water and vanished into the distance. I hoped my problems would now disappear too.

Facing New Challenges

For the most part, the summer was going wonderfully. I gained weight and got stronger by doing my therapy. But no matter how hard I tried, I couldn't bend over and touch my hands below my knees. The muscles in my legs were still pretty tight. That made my legs and back ache a lot. But I learned to take the pain in stride — most of the time anyway.

Then, toward the end of the summer, I started having bad headaches again! I was afraid something was wrong with my shunt. But my doctors said it was working perfectly. So they gave me different kinds of medicine. None of them helped much. Sometimes if I pushed real hard on my forehead, it relieved some of the pain. Lying down for a while with my healing blanket over my head seemed to help too.

When school started I was eager to see my friends. And I felt lucky that Ms. Wood would be my fourth-grade teacher. She had been my teacher in Second Grade, and we were good friends. But I wondered if I was ready to attend classes every day. I still tired easily and had headaches. Noises and bright lights continued to bother me.

Adam was probably the brightest and most creative child I had ever had in my second-grade class. He could draw anything. And he would catch on to jokes that other second graders didn't understand. Everything came easily to him. While the other students were struggling with addition and subtraction, Adam already knew his multiplication tables. He was also the class clown. All of these qualities made him very popular with his classmates.

Jeri Wood
Second and Fourth Grade Teacher

27

And I worried that I might get upset and cry in front of my classmates. I certainly didn't want that to happen.

The first few weeks of school were really difficult. I tried my best to do everything right, but I kept having headaches. When the headaches were really bad, the school nurse, Ms. Shields, would let me lie down on the couch in her office. When the lights were turned off and the door was shut, I could finally relax. If I felt better after a while, I would return to class. But if my headache got worse, Ms. Shields would phone my mother. Mom and I would decide if I could tough it out or if she needed to come and take me home.

Mom never knew when the nurse might call. So Dad got her a beeper. Then Mom could go wherever she wanted, and I was always just a beep away. At first her beeper beeped a lot. But as my headaches went away, the beeper sounded less and less.

Trying To Gear Up

Before the accident I had never had trouble with school work. Everything always came easily to me. Now it was hard for me to do some things — especially handwriting. My mind knew the answers, but my hand wouldn't get in gear. As the days passed, I was getting farther behind.

Finally I told Mom and Dad I was having trouble with my school work. Dr. Govaerts and my parents worked out a plan with my teacher. I started going home for lunch every day to get away from all the noise. At home I could lie down and rest before finishing my lessons. To reduce the stress even more, my teacher had me do only every other problem on my math papers. And she told me I didn't have to write out all of my answers in sentences on the English papers. That really helped.

Since I now looked more like a well kid, some of my classmates had a hard time understanding why I couldn't do everything they did. When they discovered that I wasn't completing all parts of the assignments, they complained to the teacher. That hurt my feelings. So I tried even harder, and I hoped I would soon be able to handle a full load.

A Brief Update

When summer came I wanted to try playing baseball again. Before the accident it had been my best sport. I could still hit the ball pretty well. But my reflexes weren't fast enough for me to get out of the way of the wild pitches. I was hit on the arms and legs, then finally on the head. I could live with bruised arms and legs. But I didn't have to be hit in the face many times before I decided baseball was no longer my game.

When I entered the Fifth Grade, I found other things to do. I became a Safety Patrol Officer and joined the Computer Club. I now spend a lot of time on my hobbies — stamp collecting and chemistry. As for baseball, I still keep my hand in by coaching Tyler on his batting and catching.

Things To Consider

I'm glad that I can now go to school with the other kids. And I'm really happy that my handwriting has improved and that I'm able to solve math problems more easily. I don't worry much if my classmates complain about me doing every other problem. I know that I'm doing the best I can.

I can now walk well, and my running is much better. And I think the sight in my left eye is okay. But most of all — I'm thankful to be alive.

I think I've become a better person too. Since I had my accident, I have a better understanding of how handicapped people feel. When I see people in wheelchairs, I know how difficult it is for them to get around. When I see other children in the hospital, I know how hard they're working to get well. I like to visit with them. I remember how lonely it can be in a hospital room and how nice it is to have another kid to talk to.

I don't know why accidents happen, but they do. And they can happen to anyone. My parents tell me we learn from even the bad things that happen in our lives. I've thought about that and wondered what I've learned.

I think I have learned:

Accidents happen, and they can change our lives.

We can stand more pain than we think we can.

Even at the worst times, we always have a little bit of courage left inside of us.

Don't give up hope.

Never laugh when others can't do things you can do.

If you are sick, there are doctors and nurses who will try to make you well.

Teachers can be understanding and very helpful too.

When bad things happen, relatives and friends will help you in every way they can.

There are good people everywhere who care about you, even if they have never met you.

If you are going to get hurt or become sick, you are fortunate if you have a mother, a father, and two brothers who will stand by you all the way.

And...If you are carrying arrows or any sharp objects — don't fall down!

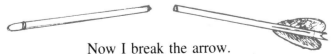

Now I break the arrow.
I hope you walk in peace and good health.

Tyler and I dressed for the '50's party at school. We thought we looked "real cool."

The four Moore boys on vacation. Front to back — Tyler, Ryan, me, and our dad Paul. (Mom was with us. She took the picture.)

THE NATIONAL WRITTEN & ILLUSTRATED

— THE 1989 NATIONAL AWARD WINNING BOOKS —

Lauren Peters
age 7

Problems at the North Pole
Written & Illustrated by Lauren Peters

the Legend of SIR MIGUEL
Written and Illustrated by MICHAEL CAIN

WE ARE A THUNDERSTORM
written and photographed by amity gaige

Michael Cain
age 11

—THE 1987 NATIONAL AWARD WINNING BOOKS—

Amity Gaige
age 16

JOSHUA DISOBEYS
Written and Illustrated by Dennis Vollmer

THE HALF & HALF DOG
written and illustrated by LISA GROSS

who owns The sun?
~written & illustrated by~ STACY CHBOSKY

Dennis Vollmer
age 6

—THE 1989 GOLD AWARD WINNERS—

BROKEN ARROW BOY
WRITTEN and ILLUSTRATED BY ADAM MOORE and his friends

GET THAT GOAT!
WRITTEN AND ILLUSTRATED BY MICHAEL AUSHENKER

Students' Winning Books Motivate and Inspire

Each year it is Landmark's pleasure to publish the winning books of The National Written & Illustrated By... Awards Contest For Students. These are important books because they supply such positive motivation and inspiration for other talented students to write and illustrate books too!

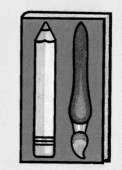

Students of All Ages Love the Winning Books

Students of all ages enjoy reading these fascinating books created by our young author/illustrators. When students see the beautiful books, printed in full color and handsomely bound in hardback covers, they, too, will become excited about writing and illustrating books and eager to enter them in the Contest.

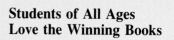

Lisa Gross
age 12

Stacy Chbosky
age 14

Adam Moore
age 9

Michael Aushenker
age 19

Enter Your Book In the Next Contest

If you are 6 to 19 years of age, you may enter the Contest too. Perhaps your book may be one of the next winners and you will become a published author and illustrator too.